TIGER SQUADRONS

DE NADA A FORTE GENTE SE TEMA
JAGUARES

F-104 S
192nci FiLO

52

230

21° GRUPPO
AD HOSTES RUGENS

142

313 SQ
SCHERPGETAND

335 MK

816

23RD TAC FTR WG

PATRON 8

430th TFS

336 SQD
TICERS

ROYAL NAVAL AIR SQUADRON
814
THE FLYING TIGERS
ROYAL NAVAL AIR SQUADRON

Staffel 11

TIGER SQUADRONS

Tim Laming

OSPREY
AEROSPACE

Published in 1991 by Osprey Publishing Limited
59 Grosvenor Street, London W1X 9DA

British Library Cataloguing in Publication Data

Laming, Tim
    Tiger squadrons. – (Osprey colour series).
    1. Air forces
    I. title
    358.4131

ISBN 1 85532 146 7

Editor Dennis Baldry
Page design Simon Ray-Hills
Printed in Hong Kong

Front cover Sporting impressive
tiger nose art, an F-4E Phantom II of
the 141st Tactical Fighter Squadron,
108th Tactical Fighter Wing, New
Jersey Air National Guard cycles the
landing gear for the benefit of the
photographer before returning to
McGuire AFB (*Tim Laming*)

Back cover A superbly painted
Puma of No 230 Sqn, RAF stays on
track for RAF Upper Heyford and the
1990 mini Tiger Meet. This unit is
the only helicopter-equipped member
of the tiger fraternity (*Howard Jones*)

Title page Tiger! Tiger! A selection
of tiger squadron badges from
around the world

Right The wild black/yellow scheme
applied by EC 5/330 of the French
Air Force to this Mirage 2000 was
short-lived!

Overleaf Tiger! Tiger! The author visited
San Diego Zoo specifically for this
book! (*Tim Laming*)

For a catalogue of all books published by Osprey Aerospace
please write to:

**The Marketing Department,
Octopus Illustrated Books, 1st Floor, Michelin House,
81 Fulham Road, London SW3 6RB**

Contents

Introduction

It all started back in 1961, when three NATO fighter squadrons assembled at RAF Woodbridge in Suffolk and hosted what became known as the 'Tiger Meet'. The year before, aircrew of the 79th Tactical Fighter Squadron, US Air Force at Woodbridge suggested the idea of creating an informal fraternity of NATO fighter units which had tigers as part of their official badges. The 79th TFS already enjoyed a close association with No 74 Sqn of the Royal Air force at nearby RAF Coltishall, and links were quickly established with *Escadre de Chasse 1/12* of *L'Armée de L'Air* based at Cambrai.

The main objectives of the Tiger Meet were to encourage professional relationships between NATO squadrons and foster solidarity within the air forces of the alliance. Thirty years on, NATO is still very much in business; all of the original tiger squadrons remain operational, their numbers swollen by many new units, including some from outside Europe. Whenever possible tiger squadrons come together as a team, discuss their varied operational roles and continue the spirit of friendship.

The original aim of this book was to take a close look at just some of today's tiger squadrons, but as I began to delve more deeply into the subject it became clear that the sheer variety of combat aircraft and their often bizarre colour schemes meant that a more comprehensive treatment of the subject was required. However, without the aid of a time machine and an unlimited travel expenses account, the task was simply beyond my resources alone. Thankfully, I was able to count on the co-operation of a large number of individuals who were just as keen to contribute to the history of the tiger squadrons.

It is impossible to thank everyone who assisted and those who gave so freely of their time and colour transparencies, but some of the main players were Kai Anders, Grivel Arnaud, Chris Bennett, Geraldo Estevans (Portuguese AF); Giuseppe Fassari, Christian Gerard, John Hale, Arild Heiestad (Royal Norwegian AF); Michael Hill (RAF Strike Command); Andy Hodgson, Paul Hoehn, Gordon James (No 74 Sqn, RAF); Howard Jones (No 230 Sqn, RAF); Don Matthews (No 439 Sqn, CAF); Willy Scheungrab (AG-52, *Luftwaffe*); Robbie Shaw, Pal Simonsen (Royal Norwegian AF); Luca Storti, David Swearingen (New Jersey ANG); Frank Visser and Rembert Vornholz.

I hope everyone will enjoy the results of our collective efforts.

Tim Laming
Sheffield 1991

United States Air Force

Left Descending through patchy cloud cover, a McDonnell Douglas F-4E Phantom II multi-role fighter of the 141st Tactical Fighter Squadron, 108th Tactical Fighter Wing, New Jersey Air National Guard heads for the bombing range. The F-4E may be an old lady, but she's no slouch when it comes to delivering a powerful punch to a ground target. From the back seat the attack looked impressive enough, but the folks in the range tower must have got a marvellous view as the Phantoms thundered by at 50 ft, afterburners blazing against the evening sky (*Tim Laming*)

Right On the ground at McGuire AFB everything was looking good ... your intrepid correspondent was settled into the back seat and the J79 turbojets were energized. But the communications just didn't want to know. After a careful discussion over the R/T, it was decided that our wingman would wait for us while the ground crew attempted a quick fix. Then the crew chief appeared ... and the news was bad. The offending 'black box' was directly under the author's seat. So the engines are wound down, the canopies are opened, and the crew vacate the aircraft while the problem is solved. Standing on a Phantom's fuselage in a New Jersey winter ain't much fun, but the technician does his job (*Tim Laming*)

Right The wheels just lifting off the concrete at McGuire AFB, an F-4E of the 108th TFW gets airborne with a full load of blue-painted inert practice bombs. The 'Wizzo' (Weapons Systems Officer) in the back seat is probably smiling for the camera, but the oxygen mask tends to spoil the effect. The flamboyant tiger motif certainly doesn't look too friendly! Once the landing gear and flaps are retracted, it's time for a smart right turn out to the east, en route for the weapons range (*Tim Laming*)

Below Above the clouds, the winter sunshine highlights the drab 'European One' camouflage scheme of F-4E 68-386. Most of the 108th TFW's F-4Es are painted in 'Egyptian One' tactical greys, however, and they are likely to retain this scheme for the rest of their careers, at the end of which the wing will have transitioned to the F-16 Fighting Falcon. Both the 141st TFS and 177th FIS of the New Jersey ANG will be re-equipped with F-16s, the latter squadron having already 'traded-in' their F-106 Delta Darts for A model Fighting Falcons at Atlantic City Airport—'just down the road' from McGuire AFB in New Jersey (*Tim Laming*)

Also featured on the front cover, this carefully timed break allows a good look at the Phantom's landing gear retraction sequence. The F-4E model's leading edge slats, retrofitted in the early 1970s to reduce turn radius and improve overall manoeuvrability—at the expense of rarely needed Mach 2 capability—are also clearly visible (*Tim Laming*)

Left Sheltered from the bleak winter temperatures in the middle of the Fort Dix Military Reservation, the 141st TFS maintenance hangar provides the ground crews with a shirtsleeve environment in which the ageing F-4E's can be given the increasingly large amounts of attention they demand. The 141st TFS Bengal Tiger motif is visible on the left intake (*Tim Laming*)

Overleaf On long final approach to McGuire, with Lockheed C-141 Starlifters and Boeing KC-135 Stratotankers ahead of us, the clouds sweep up to envelope the canopy, inserting our Phantom into the early evening gloom. Just below us is Lakehurst NAS, the infamous site of the giant German airship *Hindenburg's* fiery demise. Soon there will be a brightly lit runway, a welcoming ground crew and a warm bar—hopefully in that order (*Tim Laming*)

Above If you close your eyes and imagine yourself moving back in time, it's not so hard to picture the days when the McGuire flight line was graced with the presence of F-4D Phantom II fighter-bombers. And at nearby Atlantic City, the 141st's sister squadron was still flying F-106 Delta Darts (*Tim Laming*)

Above Kleine Brogel, Belgium in 1987, and the 393rd Bomb Squadron of Strategic Air Command, based at Pease AFB in New Hampshire, flew this eye-catcher to the Tiger Meet—complete with decorated tail, old-style Southeast Asia camouflage and the 'SAC band' around the nose. The squadron's FB-111As have since been re-assigned to Tactical Air Command as F-111Gs (*Kai Anders*)

Right Underside view of an FB-111A from the 393rd BS performing at the 1989 International Air Tattoo at RAF Fairford in Gloucestershire—part of the 'SAC Attack' during the show (*Tim Laming*)

An official 'Tiger Club' member since 1968, the 393rd BS fell victim to US budget cuts and was disbanded in 1990; Pease AFB was closed and the tigers may well have seen the last of the 393rd (*Tim Laming*)

Where it all started; the 79th TFS is credited with the original idea of setting up a tiger fraternity way back in 1960. Still very much in business at RAF Upper Heyford in Oxfordshire, the squadron is part of the 20th TFW and operates the F-111E. Ship 68-002 displays early white tail codes, now applied in black (*Andy Hodgson Collection*)

Left The tiger-striped fin top identifies this F-111E as a 79th TFS aircraft. Flaps and slats are fully extended, and the tailerons are fully deflected as the big swinger rumbles along the runway on her landing roll out. Two AIM-9 Sidewinders mounted on the inner weapons pylons give the F-111 a self-defence capability (*Kai Anders*)

Above The 79th TFS has been deployed in the UK since 1943, operating P-38 Lightnings and P-51 Mustangs until the end of World War 2. Post-war, the squadron operated the F-84G Thunderjet and F-84F Thunderstreak before transitioning to the F-100D/F Super Sabre, which remained in service until the F-111 'Aardvarks' arrived in 1970. The F-111Es are expected to remain at Upper Heyford for a long time, unless conventional/nuclear arms talks dictate otherwise (*Tim Laming*)

An F-15D combat-capable trainer of the 53rd TFS, United States Air Forces Europe, on final approach to its base at Bitburg in Germany. Apart from the centreline fuel tank. This 'twin-stick' Eagle is in clean configuration—or is it? There's a Sidewinder AAM up there somewhere (*Christian Gerard/VDL*)

Positioned in front of Bitburg's control tower, an F-15A Eagle air superiority fighter of the 53rd TFS stands ready. A long-time participant at annual Tiger Meets, the squadron operated the F-105 Thunderchief, F-4D and F-4E Phantom IIs before re-equipping with the McDonnell Douglas F-15 Eagle in 1977. The 53rd TFS is one of four US Air Force air defence squadrons permanently based in Europe

Above What the Eagle pilot wears; the parachute and seat harness attachments are visible, as is the connection hose for the anti-G suit (the 'speed jeans'). Once the aircraft is signed away, it's time to fly. Anyone for an air combat manoeuvring (ACM) hop? (*Chris Bennett*)

Left An Eagle at rest outside a Tab Vee bomb-proof shelter at Bitburg AB (*Chris Bennett*)

Above Never great enthusiasts for exotic colour schemes, the 53rd's best attempt at tiger markings so far has been this tastefully decorated F-15A. But maybe when you're operating the most potent fighter around, you don't have to worry about fancy paint schemes? (*Kai Anders*)

Left A 53rd TFS F-15 pilot prepares for a duel of Eagles (*Chris Bennett*)

Left The Fairchild A-10 Thunderbolt II will forever be known by aircrew and groundcrew as the 'Warthog' It's not difficult to see why, as from every imaginable angle this aeroplane spells UGLY. The 23rd TFW didn't try to make their 'Hogs look pretty: they made them look even more fearsome by adding sharkmouths above the aircraft's mighty 30 mm Avenger cannon. It was with the 23rd TFW that the Warthog received its baptism of fire, attacking Iraqi army positions in Kuwait during the Gulf War (*Paul Hoehn*)

Above Loaded with two 600 US gal ferry tanks, this A-10 is ready to make the long trip home; from England to England, as the 23rd TFW's operating base is England AFB in Louisiana (*Paul Hoehn*)

Before converting to the A-10, the 23rd TFW operated the Vought A-7D. To you and me that's a Corsair II, but it's worth noting that unlike the US Navy, the US Air Force has never formally adopted the name 'Corsair' for their A-7s. The unit's traditional sharkmouth markings survived the transition to the 'Hog; alas, the Southeast Asia 'Vietnam' camouflage didn't (*Paul Hoehn*)

United States Navy

Based at Brunswick Naval Air Station in Maine, VP-8 is a recognized tiger squadron, but is not a regular visitor to annual Tiger Meets. As part of Patrol Wing Five, the unit operates the Lockheed P-3C Orion maritime patrol/anti-submarine warfare aircraft. The stylish tiger markings on the tail are long gone, however, as the US Navy decided to remove all markings (other than national insignia) during the late 1980s. So one Orion looks pretty much like any other these days, which is a great pity—flamboyant markings have always played an important part in engendering a sense of pride within individual Navy squadrons (*Frank Visser*)

Royal Air Force

Left A Phantom pilot of No 74 ('Tiger') Sqn expresses himself as only fighter pilots can. This particular F-4J has a famous past: before being transferred to the RAF in 1984, she was operated by the US Navy from Pt Mugu NAS as VX-4's all-black 'Vandy One'. More than one photographer still hopes (probably in vain) that this F-4 will recover her gloss black colour scheme before being retired (*Tim Laming*)

Right Over the moon? Well, not quite, but the view is certainly unusual, as our wingman makes a close-in left turn for the cameraman's benefit. By this stage of the flight your faithful author was beginning to regret that he hadn't been feeling exactly 100 per cent before take-off. And now his resolve was starting to crack, encouraged by the stink of a rubber oxygen mask, a hot immersion suit, a heavy helmet, constant G-force and a flight path which was far from straight and level. Flights in fast jets are rarely 'joyrides'; for much of the time, even for a passenger, it's just plain hard work. Honest! (*Tim Laming*)

Above left a close-up view of the famous tiger markings as applied below the cockpit canopies of No 74 Sqn's F-4Js. Sadly, the impending retirement of the RAF's remaining Phantoms means that the squadron will probably have to disband until deliveries of the 'Eurofighter' begin in the late 1990s or (more likely) the beginning of the 21st Century (*Tim Laming*)

Below left En route to the North Sea, a look down at our wingman reveals the multi-hued camouflage applied to the F-4J's upper surfaces. It looks green and it *is* green, despite being supposed to be air defence grey. The paint was applied in the US (to RAF specifications) before delivery; unfortunately, somewhere along the line, the paint didn't quite appear in the correct shade (*Tim Laming*)

Right One of No 74 Sqn's 'Juliet' model F-4s takes a brief rest inside a Hardened Aircraft Shelter (HAS) At the unit's home base at RAF Wattisham in Suffolk. These concrete mini-hangars are designed to protect the Phantoms from all manner of destructive power, but they are not airtight—as witnessed by the jet exhaust ducts visible behind the aircraft. Consequently, every time the air raid sirens sound, aircrews and groundcrews have to don Nuclear-Biological-Chemical (NBC) protection(*Tim Laming*)

Above Back in Wattisham's pattern, Phantom ZE359/'J' lowers the flaps and landing gear for a right turn onto final approach. Unencumbered by external stores (apart from a single Sidewinder acquisition round) this F-4J displayed awesome acceleration during air combat manoeuvring (ACM) (*Tim Laming*)

Left Joining-up before tanking, two of these Phantoms display the standard F-4J fit of one centreline fuel tank—a noticeably different configuration from the RAF's anglicized F-4K/M models, which usually carry two underwing tanks. The black fins are a fairly recent concession to squadron history, and recall the days of their similarly decorated English Electric Lightnings (*Tim Laming*)

Above The view from Phantom ZE355/'S' as a trio of F-4Js take-on fuel from a Lockheed TriStar of No 216 Sqn at 25,000 feet over the North Sea in April 1990. Once everyone is 'topped-up', it's down to 250 ft over the snow covered hills of northern England for a 2 v 2 ACM exercise (*Tim Laming*)

Left Heading towards RAF Leeming in North Yorkshire, where the crews of the Tornado Fighter Wing are eagerly wating for some passing 'trade', the rear-seat Wizzo's (Navigators in RAF-speak) are keeping a watchful eye on their radar screens for any signs of activity. A hard break, followed by a steep descent, takes the Tigers down from the smooth air at high altitudes into the bumpy, gut-wrenching environment of low-level air defence. Time to get intimate with those hills (*Tim Laming*)

Above No 74 Sqn was one of the 'founding fathers' of the tiger fraternity. Equipped with Lightning interceptors at RAF Coltishall in Norfolk, the Tigers enjoyed excellent relations with the US Air force's 79th TFS at nearby RAF Woodbridge; in 1961 the squadrons assembled at Woodbridge in company with the Frenchmen of EC.1/12 to create the first Tiger Meet. Alas, the slow demise of the Lightning saw the disbandment of No 74 Sqn in August 1971 at RAF Tengah, Singapore and it wasn't until 1984 that the Tigers reformed at Wattisham with refurbished F-4Js from the US Navy. By January 1991, No 74 Sqn had retired its F-4Js after receiving Phantom FGR.2s (F-4Ms) released by the two redundant RAF air defence squadrons in Germany (*Tim Laming*)

Right You don't have to fly a fast jet to be a tiger. No 230 Sqn operates the Aérospatiale/Westland Puma helicopter and is mostly tasked with supporting the British Army in the field. One of the RAF's oldest operational squadrons, No 230 has participated in Tiger Meets since 1977, maintaining the sole RAF presence at the event until No 74 Sqn reformed in 1984. Their Pumas are still regular and reliable participants at Tiger Meets; during 1990 No 230 Sqn provided the year's tiger-striped aircraft (*Howard Jones*)

Left Back in 1982 Puma XW229 wore this attractive black/yellow paint scheme. Following Iraq's invasion of Kuwait in August 1990, most of No 230 Sqn's Pumas received applications of desert pink paint before they were deployed to the Gulf in support of British land forces (*Kai Anders*)

Above Puma 'Delta Papa', in normal tactical camouflage, still proudly displays No 230 Sqn's tiger spirit with some superb artwork on the nose fairing. The lower appendages are believed to be a radar warning receiver (RWR) and a spotlight (*Paul Hoehn*)

Royal Navy – Fleet Air Arm

Based at RNAS Culdrose in Cornwall and operating from the aircraft carriers HMS *Invincible, Illustrious* and *Ark Royal* as required, No 814 Naval Air Squadron is the Royal Navy's only tiger unit. Tasked with anti-submarine warfare duties, No 814 NAS is equipped with the Westland Sea King HAS.5 helicopter; XV665 is pictured on static display at RAF Mildenhall in May 1986 (*John Hale*)

L'Armée de l'Air

Right The 1977 International Air Tattoo at RAF Greenham Common in Berkshire saw a public gathering of tiger squadrons. *Escadre de Chasse* 1/12 provided a very smart black/yellow Dassault Super Mystère B.2 fighter-bomber, which took part in the weekend flying display. Plenty has happened since those heady days: the Super Mystères have all been withdrawn; RAF Greenham Common saw the arrival and, after successful intermediate nuclear force (INF) reduction talks between NATO and the Soviet Union, the departure of Tomahawk cruise missiles; and the bi-annual International Air Tattoo has moved to RAF Fairford in Gloucestershire (*Kai Anders*)

Below EC1/12 participated in the now famous initial Tiger Meet at RAF Woodbridge in 1961 and their links with the tiger fraternity are consequently long and proud. Formed in 1918, the unit was originally known as *Escadrille SPA 162*. In 1953 the unit was reformed as a twin-escadrille *'Escadre de Chasse'* (fighter wing) at Cambrai, Equipped with Dassault Ouragans and later the Mystère IV and Super Mystère, EC1/12 received its first Mirage F.1C fighters in 1977. In the 1970s the unit markings were applied to the fin (vertical stabilizer) with typical French panache. But in common with other air forces, *L'Armée de l'Air* encouraged the application of low-vis markings during the 1980s

Unlike many of their NATO counterparts, EC1/12 has not completely tiger-striped any of their aircraft since they operated the Super Mystére. The nearest the unit have come (so far) to adorning a Mirage F.1 in such colours was 12-YE, which appeared at the 1979 Tiger Meet. Close examination of this photo will reveal that members of No 439 Sqn, Canadian Armed forces have already visited this Mirage with a paint brush (*Paul Hoehn*)

Up above the clouds in its natural element the sleek Mirage F.1 looks every
inch a fighter. Built-in armament is a pair of 30 mm DEFA cannon (each with
135 rounds of usually high-explosive ammunition), and the missile mix is
typically two wingtip Matra R.550 Magic infrared-guided AAMs, and/or two
Matra Super 530F radar-guided AAMs. The bolt-on flight refuelling probe is
only fitted when a mission requires tanker support. If you've a head for figures,
you might care to note that the engine is a SNECMA Atar 9K-50 turbojet with
a maximum (afterburner) thrust of 15,873 lb at sea level. Although not in the
same class as the F-16 or Mirage 2000, the F.1 is capable of taking off after a
ground roll of just over 2000 ft, climbing to an altitude of 65,000 ft and
reaching speeds in excess of Mach 2 (*SIRPA-AIR*)

Above Days of dullness: the yellow outline to the national insignia has disappeared, the yellow component of the walkway demarkation lines went too, and the beautiful fin markings were reduced to graffiti. It's possibly a rather sad way to treat an object of great pride, but the tactics of modern aerial warfare dictate that small is beautiful when it comes to unit and national markings. In a shooting war (such as in the Gulf in 1991) most unit markings are over-sprayed with camouflage paint (*Kai Anders*)

Right Another two-seat Mirage F.1B combat-capable trainer, also wearing the markings of EC5/330 'Cote d'Argent' (*Grivel Arnaud*)

In case there was any doubt as to what EC5/330's unit emblem looked like, they painted it on one of their Mirage 2000s—and they painted it big! Mirage 330-AH presents a near-perfect platform during a flight from her home base at Mont-de-Marsan. EC5/330 is a recent addition to the Tiger Meet participation list (*SIRPA-AIR*)

Left Leading edge slats extended, a Mirage 2000 performs a long, low, slow pass for the benefit of an airshow audience. Superficially similar to the famed Mirage III, the 2000 is in fact a completely new design featuring an aerodynamically advanced delta wing and fly-by-wire controls (*Tim Laming*)

Above right Mirage 2000B combat-capable trainer of EC5/330 pictured during a courtesy visit to a fellow tiger squadron at Kleine Brogel in Belgium. The pilot of 330-AX is wearing a helmet which leaves one in no doubt as to which squadron he flies with (*Christian Gerard/VDL*)

Below right A Mirage 2000N (Nuclear) strike aircraft of EC5/330 resplendent in grey/green low-level tactical camouflage and carrying a pair of massive underwing fuel tanks (*Grivel Arnaud*)

Aéronautique Navale

Demonstrating the manoeuvrability of Dassault-Breguet's attractive naval strike fighter, a pilot of *Flottille* 11F heaves his Super Etendard out of a loop, squeezing streams of condensation out of the summer sky (*Tim Laming*)

In 1986, *Flottille* 11F gave one of their Super Etendards the tiger treatment. With typical French artistic flair and taste, 11F produced a beautiful tiger emblem under the cockpit canopy and made a minor but effective modification to the code letters and numbers, which are normally painted white (*Christian Gerard/VDL*)

Flottille 11F of the French Navy is shore based at Landivisiau in northern France and operates from the aircraft carrier *Clemenceau* as required. The unit badge features a sea horse—not quite a tiger, but someone discovered that the official emblem of the warship is indeed a tiger. The rest is history. Wrap-around camouflage is now standard on the unit's Super Etendards (*Tim Laming*)

Force Aérienne Belge/Belgische Luchtmacht

Yep, they did it too! The 31st *Smaldeel* of the Belgian Air Force are past masters of tiger stripery, as demonstrated by one of the unit's Lockheed F-104G Starfighters during the 1978 Tiger Meet. To achieve this stunning effect hard-edged black stripes were painted over an orange-yellow base colour (*via Kai Anders*)

Left The Starfighters may be gone, but memories remain in tangible form outside the 31st *Smaldeel's* offices at Kleine Brogel, where an F-104 wingtip fuel tank is decorated with a list of former squadron commanders and the aircraft types operated by the unit (*Frank Visser*)

Above right Before they converted to the Starfighter, the 31st *Smaldeel* operated the Republic F-84F Thunderstreak; one such example, coded 8S-H, is preserved at Kleine Brogel. The squadron attended their first Tiger Meet with the F-84F (*Frank Visser*)

Below right The 31st *Smaldeel* operated the F-104G Starfighter from 1964 until 1982, when the first F-16s arrived at Kleine Brogel. US Air Force-style camouflage was peculiar to Belgian Starfighters (*Andy Hodgson Collection*)

Above F-16A FA-62 was without a doubt the star attraction at the 25th anniversary Tiger Meet held at Kleine Brogel in 1985. The sensitive nature of the anti-radar paint meant that the Fighting Falcon had to be decorated using coloured latex. And it didn't come cheap, costing the squadron some $1300! But everyone agreed that the result was worth every cent—a real show-stopper! Wisely, the latex wasn't applied forward of the jet intake, as it was feared the stuff would peel off in flight and be ingested by the engine. Sure enough, after FA-62's one-and-only flight in its tiger markings, large chunks of latex parted company with the airframe, never to be seen again . . . (*Andy Hodgson Collection*)

Left Love it or hate it (every pilot adores it!), the General Dynamics F-16 Fighting Falcon is a multi-role fighter to be reckoned with. The F-16 is wickedly manoeuvrable, as demonstrated by this tight, low-level turn, vortices streaming off the leading edge extensions (LEX). Ouch . . . you can almost feel those 9 Gs! (*Tim Laming*)

Rather more mundane, FA-72 sits on the Cambrai flight line during the 1986 Tiger Meet wearing the standard Belgian air force camouflage scheme (indeed, the almost universal F-16 colour scheme). At least the intake cover adds a dash of colour (*Christian Gerard/VDL*)

Two Fighting Falcons from the 31st *Smaldeel*, Belgian Air Force, about to depart from their home base at Kleine Brogel. The wingman looks across the leader on his right, and with a nod of confirmation the brakes are released in unison (usually), followed by a blast of power from the F-16's Pratt & Whitney F100 turbofan. The blue fin marking is that of the 10th Fighter Bomber Wing, of which the 31st is a component squadron. Having first attended a Tiger Meet in 1962, the squadron has been a regular participant in tiger events ever since (*Frank Visser*)

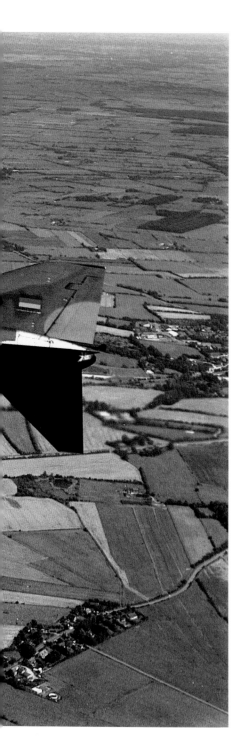

Luftwaffe

Left *Aufklarungsgeschwader* 52 (or simply 'AG-52') is better known as the 52nd Tactical Reconnaissance Wing, based at Leck. Formed in 1959, the wing comprises two RF-4E squadrons: 521 and 522. Although both units attend Tiger Meets, it is No 521 which is the 'official' tiger squadron. Assigned to NATO in 1963, AG-52 moved from its initial base at Erding, via Eggebeck, to their present home at Leck in 1971 (*Willy Scheungrab*)

Above High over Schleswig Holstein in March 1990, this close-up of an RF-4E Phantom II from AG-52 reveals the low-vis emblem applied to the jet intake: a black panther with camera shutter strips and the wing number. The nose camera windows are visible; additional transparencies are incorporated into the underside of the nose (*Willy Scheungrab*)

Left Inside 521's reception hall there's an unmistakeable reminder of the past in the shape of an RF-104G tailplane—suitably adorned with a beautiful tiger design. Cat lovers are guaranteed to enjoy a tour of any tiger squadron crew room! (*Willy Scheungrab*)

Above The *Luftwaffe* does not have any tanker aircraft at present, so flight refuelling is provided by the US Air Force. Two RF-4Es of AG-52 take on fuel from a Boeing KC-135A 'Stratobladder' at 25,000 ft over Germany (*Willy Scheungrab*)

Above Back in 1959, AG-52 flew the RF-84 Thunderflash; a solitary example of this fine aircraft remains on display at Leck AB. In 1964 the first RF-104G Starfighters arrived and the unit remained operational on the photo-recce version of Lockheed's 'manned missile' until the RF-4E Phantom IIs were delivered in 1971 (*Willy Scheungrab*)

Left They say you should never work with children or animals. As a cat owner, the author knows that this advice is particularly true in the case of our feline friends. Group photographs are a good idea, but keeping control of nine AG-52 tiger aircrew is rather difficult. The addition of two members of the unofficial groundcrew didn't exactly help. You ever tried asking a cat to smile? (*Kai Anders*)

Right Variations on the black/yellow theme are many, but one of the most noteworthy is this striking colour scheme applied to one of AG-52's RF-4Es (35 + 76) in 1984. The unit expects to be flying their Phantoms until at least 1994, when Panavia Tornados are scheduled to assume the reconnaissance task (*Kai Anders*)

Above When 431 *Staffel/Jagdbomber-Geschwader* 43 attended their first Tiger Meet in 1963, they were mounted on the classic Canadair Sabre—a hugely popular jet fighter. This Sabre is preserved atop a display plinth at Oldenburg. Although the *JaboG* 43 emblem is visible, 431 *Staffel's* **fox head** badge isn't. Not surprisingly, when the unit first came to the Meet, their eligibility for 'tigership' was questioned. One of 431's pilots reportedly said, '*Believe it or not, this emblem is a tiger*'. After the unit displayed that kind of nerve, nobody had the heart to turn them away! (*Kai Anders*)

Above In 1967 the Sabres were retired and *JaboG* 43 re-equipped with the Fiat G.91R, plus a handfull of G-91T two-seat trainers. Until 1981, when the Alpha Jets arrived, the colourful 'Ginas' were present at every Tiger Meet (*Kai Anders*)

Right The MBB-built Stencel S-111-S3AJ ejection seat enabled this particular Alpha Jet pilot to survive a mid-air collision with an RAF Tornado. In common with the Martin-Baker Mk 10 design fitted to other Alpha Jets, the Stencel seat has zero-zero capability (*Kai Anders*)

Above The bright international orange flying suit of this *Luftwaffe* pilot contrasts with the green/grey camouflage worn by his Alpha Jet. In wartime, the *Luftwaffe* would issue 'low-vis' flying clothing to its aircrews (*Kai Anders*)

Right Engine test: foreign object damage (FOD) guard safely in place, the ground crew prepare to start the Alpha Jet's two SNECMA/Turbomeca Larzac 04-C6 turbofan engines, each rated at 2976 lb of thrust at sea level (*Kai Anders*)

The *Luftwaffe* has gradually applied a highly effective 'Lizard' camouflage scheme to its fleet of Alpha Jet attack aircraft (*Christian Gerard/VDL*)

JaboG 43 celebrated its 25th anniversary on 10 November 1984; in traditional *Luftwaffe* fashion, one of the unit's Alpha Jets (40 + 44) received a commemorative colour scheme. Being the wing's celebration (rather than the *staffel's*), there wasn't a trace of a tiger stripe anywhere on the aircraft! (*Kai Anders*)

Forca Aerea Portuguese

The venerable Fiat G.91R attack aircraft is operated by 301 *Esquadra* based at Motijo airbase in Portugal. The unit saw combat during the guerilla war in Mozambique (which was a Portuguese colony). With its distinctive nose profile, the 'Gina' has been in NATO service for nearly 25 years (*Kai Anders*)

Left The tail-mounted braking parachute has yet to be properly repacked into the housing on G.91 number 5466, as the drogue portion is still flapping defiantly in the warm Portuguese breeze. The standard brown/green camouflage scheme used by the Portuguese air force is also displayed by the Lockheed C-130 Hercules taxying in the background (*Kai Anders*)

Above As if there was any doubt that 301 *Esquadra* 'Jaguares' was a true tiger squadron the 1987 Meet saw the traditional application of black and yellow paint to one of their G.91Rs. The result was, to say the least, impressive (*Rembert Vornholz/VDL*)

Left A closer view of the cockpit area reveals the dual-language instructions and the 301 *Esquadra* emblem. Strictly speaking, the squadron isn't a tiger unit as their badge features a jaguar. But we're not going to split feline hairs: a cat is a cat, right? Certainly the pilot has got the tiger spirit, as witnessed by his very stylish bone dome (*Kai Anders*)

Above After being retired from *Luftwaffe* service, batches of G.91s were delivered to Portugal and retained their grey/green camouflage. The G.91 has a built-in armament of four 12.7 mm Colt-Browning machine guns; Sidewinder AAMs and a variety of ground attack stores can be carried underwing. Alpha Jets are expected to replace the Ginas during the course of 1991 (*Kai Anders*)

The G.91T two-seat trainer retains the same Orpheus turbojet as fitted to the single-seat Gina. Derived from the North American F-86 Sabre, the G.91 was developed as a direct result of a joint NATO requirement for a light fighter and tactical support aircraft issued in 1953. So who said the 'Eurofighter' was a new idea? (*Frank Visser*)

This Vought A-7P Corsair II belongs to 304 *Esquadra*; judging by the badge on the fin, 304 is at least an 'unofficial' tiger squadron. However, the word is that when the G.91s are finally withdrawn from service, this unit may well assume the role of being Portugal's official tiger squadron. I wonder if we will see a tiger-striped Corsair? (*Frank Visser*)

Ejercito del Air

Left Equipped with Mirage F.1CEs and F.1BE two-seaters, *Escuadron* 142 of the Spanish air force is based at Los Llanos airbase, southeast of Madrid. This F.1BE is taxying out for take-off during squadron exchange in Germany (*Marcus Gehrlein*)

Above Primarily an air defence squadron, 142's Mirage F.1s can switch over to the ground attack role if required. This unit attended their first Tiger Meet at Cambrai in 1986. The colourful camouflage is fast disappearing in favour of air defence greys (yeuch!), but hopefully the tiger tails will be retained (*Marcus Gehrlein*)

Aeronautica Militare Italiano

Here they come! There's absolutely no mistaking these hot rods — Starfighters, in this case F-104S interceptors of 21° *Gruppo* howling into the circuit before they land at Cameri, their home base. Unless afterburner is selected, the Starfighter's trusty General Electric J79 turbojet tends to leave a tell-tale smoke trail (*Tim Laming*)

Above Nose-on view of the F-104S, emphasizing the extremely small frontal area of this distinctive design. The underwing weapons stations are for Sparrow or Aspide medium-range, radar-guided AAMs (the 'S' denotes 'Sparrow'). The wet concrete is due to the attentions of a diligent RAF fire crew who hosed down some excess fuel from under the aircraft (*Tim Laming*)

Right The 21° *Gruppo* has been a member of the exclusive tiger community since 1968; the unit has always been a Starfighter operator (initially on the G model from 1967 until 1970) during its association with the Tiger Meet (*Paul Hoehn*)

Wow! In 1988 the Tiger Meet was held at Cameri, and as the host unit 21°
Gruppo was determined to impress. this spectacular scheme duly appeared on
one of their many Starfighters (*Giuseppe Fassari*)

Outside 21° *Gruppo's* officers, an F-104G strikes a sub-orbital pose wearing the colour scheme introduced at the 1988 Tiger Meet (*Giuseppe Fassari*)

Left As this F-104S proceeds to the active runway, the underwing stores still have their safety pins attached; they will be removed during the pre-take-off checks near the runway. The leading edge of the Starfighter's wing is appropriately yellow-painted; it is actually a replacement component finished in primer paint (*Giuseppe Fassari*)

Above Those Italians, forever fashion sensitive, just had to have matching tiger road transport for their squadron. Even the ear defenders are painted to match the designer livery. If it ain't tiger striped, it just isn't cool, man! (*Giuseppe Fassari*)

Above The latest low-vis colours for Italy's Starfighters; the unit emblem has so far escaped the tone-down exercise. The huge white fuselage 'buzz numbers' are gone, replaced by blue numbers with black surrounds. The fin markings are in black outline form (*Giuseppe Fassari*)

Right Equipped with the full fit of external fuel tanks, this F-104S is temporarily without serials or unit markings. The upgraded S model's beyond visual range (BVR) kill capability, swift rate of climb, rapid acceleration and Mach 2 performance will continue to be exploited by the Italian air force until the 'Eurofighter' is ready (*Tim Laming*)

Turk Hava Kuvvetleri

The Turkish Air force also operates a large fleet of F-104s, including S models. Aircraft 2072 of the 192 *Filo* is an ex-*Luftwaffe* F-104G, as revealed by the green/grey splinter camouflage and dayglo wingtip tanks. The Turks have yet to acquire their fair share if involvement in tiger activities and 192 *Filo* are rarely seen at other NATO airbases, which is a great shame, especially if you happen to be a Starfighter addict (*Robbie Shaw*)

Elliniki Aeroporia

Once upon time, the vast majority of NATO's front-line fighter-bomber squadrons were equipped with the Lockheed F-104G Starfighter. Consequently, more than a little space on the Tiger Meet ramps was occupied by various Starfighters from different countries; although the F-104 is slowly fading into history, no less than three tiger squadrons continued to operate the type in 1991. Based at Araxos, one such unti is 335 *Mira* of the Greek Air Force. Despite having joined the tiger fraternity in 1972, the unit has rarely attended annual Tiger Meets. But 335 *Mira* have occasionally displayed some tiger spirit: check out the stripey tales trapped under the canopies of this TF-104G combat trainer (*Paul Hoehn*)

Swiss Air Force

Above Tiger Tiger: *Flieger Staffel* 11 of the Swiss Air force is not only a tiger squadron, it is also the only operator of Tiger (II) aircraft within the tiger fraternity, the name having been adopted by Northrop for their F-5E fighter. Dubendorf's single aircraft blast shelters can be seen in the distance as this Tiger II taxies back to the flight line. This roadside viewpoint is popular with enthusiasts, who are keen to see Tiger IIs and Hawker Hunters, plus the odd Junkers Ju-52, roll by (*Paul Hoehn*)

Right *Flieger Staffel* 11 is a recognized member of the tiger fraternity and their pilots regularly attend Tiger Meets; however, due to strict Swiss neutrality laws, the *staffel's* Tiger IIs are not permitted to accompany them. The nearest F-5E bears the famous tiger motif, while the second aircraft carries the markings of another Swiss Air Force tiger unit (*Tim Laming*)

A tiger member since 1981, *Staffel* 11 is based at Dubendorf AB just outside the city of Zurich. Orange-coloured Sidewinder drill rounds are usually fitted for training flights in order to familiarize pilots with the handling of the fighter in operational configuration (*Paul Hoehn*)

Royal Norwegian Air Force

Right The Royal Norwegian Air Force's distinctive national marking is displayed by this Northrop F-5A Freedom Fighter of No 336 Sqn, based at Rygge AB. In 1984, No 336 Sqn re-equipped with the F-16 Fighting Falcon but, uniquely, they re-converted back to the F-5 a year later as a tactical fighter lead-in training unit (*Tim Laming*)

Far right The Freedom Fighters of No 336 Sqn also have an electronic countermeasures (ECM) training role, as revealed by the bulk chaff dispensers attached to the underwing hardpoints of aircraft number '131' (*Pal Simonsen*)

Formed in 1949, No 336 had the honour of being the first Norwegian squadron to become operational with jet aircraft (de Havilland Vampires). Later equipment included the F-84G Thunderjet and F-86 Sabre. This unit also had the distinction of operating the air force's one-and-only aerobatic team, 'The Flying Jokers', initially with the F-86 and later the F-5. One of the squadron's F-5B combat trainers shares the ramp with a *Luftwaffe* F-4F Phantom II (*Kai Anders*)

Another view of aircraft number 131, this time as it hugs the harsh mountainous terrain in northern Norway. The sprayed aluminium colour scheme has since been replaced by gloss light greys (*Pal Simonsen*)

Koninklijke Luchtmacht

Below No 313 Sqn of the Royal Netherlands Air Force is the latest addition to the tiger family, attending their first mini Tiger Meet at RAF Upper Heyford in Oxfordshire in 1990. In common with the squadrons of many NATO air forces, No 313 are enthusiastic operators of the F-16 'Electric Jet'. The McDonnell Douglas ACES II ejection seat is permanently raked at 30 degrees in an attempt to improve the pilot's G-tolerance in air combat (*Frank Visser*)

Right The squadron's new tiger badge is visible on the fin of this Fighting Falcon. Before converting the F-16, No 313 Sqn operated the NF-5A/B Freedom Fighter (*Frank Visser*)

1.PUSH BUTTON TO OPEN DOOR
2.PULL RING OUT 6 FEET TO

Canadian Armed forces (Air)

Left A McDonnell Douglas CF-18 Hornet of No 439 Sqn based at Baden Sollingen in Germany tracks a Belgian F-16 during a dissimilar air combat training (DACT) mission over central Europe (*Roels Antoine*)

Below Flaps and slats extended, gear down, a two-ship element of multi-role CF-18s return to Baden Sollingen. No 439 Sqn is part of the 1st Canadian Air Group, and operates alongside two other CF-18 squadrons (Nos 409 and 421) from Baden Sollingen (*Chris Bennett*)

Above Configured for a ground attack mission, this Hornet duo is armed with CRV-7 rocket pods. No 439 Sqn had long been a 'fighter-bomber' unit, but at the end of 1990 they reverted to the pure fighter role, dedicated to the support of other ground attack forces (*Jens Schmidtgen*)

Left NATO co-operation is exemplified by this CF-18/F-16 formation. Tiger squadrons often train together even when they aren't attending Tiger Meets (*Roels Antoine*)

Due to the vagaries of aircraft availability and the nature of realistic air combat training, combat-capable trainers like this CF-18B are sometimes flown with the back seat empty. If possible, squadrons like to bring a two-seater to the Meet so that other tiger pilots have an opportunity to experience different types of aircraft (*Chris Bennett*)

May 1990, and No 439 Sqn line up in front of three CF-18s in happier times before the Tigers deployed to the Gulf during the Iraq-Kuwait crisis (*Jens Schmidtgen*)

Left Safely inside Baden Sollingen's servicing hangar, a neat line of CF-18 Hornets undergo various stages of maintenance (*Chris Bennett*)

Above Phew! Two No 439 Sqn technicians take a well earned break atop a CF-18 at Cameri, Italy in the summer of 1988. The spoof canopy painted on the Hornet's underside is designed to disguise the true orientation of the aircraft in a fast-moving visual air combat engagement (*Luca Storti*)

Ship 188922 is one of 24 CF-18B combat-capable trainers delivered to the Canadian Armed Forces. Both the CF-18A and the B model differ in detail from the standard F/A-18 Hornet operated by the US Navy and Marine Corps; a spotlight is mounted in the forward fuselage in order to visually identify aircraft at night, and a runway instrument landing system is fitted in place of its carrier equivalent (*Jens Schmidtgen*)

Baden Sollingen no longer echoes to the distinctive wail of the CF-104 Starfighter's General Electric/Orenda J79 turbojet, but there's still an atmosphere of affection for this fine aircraft. Ship 104815 is a 'standard' CF-104G, minus the rear and forward fuselage ECM fairings retrofitted to most of the Starfighters which served with the 1st Canadian Air Group. The overall green paintwork on this aircraft was something of an interim measure, spanning the years between the early natural metal schemes and the final disruptive grey/green camouflage (*Kai Anders*)

Left Back in 1979, the Canadians decorated Starfighter 104862, but decided to dispense with the white surround to the nose maple leaf emblem, thus revealing the grey/green camouflage colour beneath. Visiting crews from the RAF's No 230 Sqn evidently couldn't resist adding their own artistic touch to the nose cone (*Andy Hodgson Collection*)

Above Ship 1004761 was the 1981 'victim' for the ritual application of black/yellow paint. The Canadians first applied the scheme to a Starfighter for the 1969 Tiger Meet at RAF Woodbridge in Suffolk, and the results caused so much comment (not all of it favourable!) that tiger-striping continued until 1984. By 1985, No 439 Sqn were busy converting to the CF-18 Hornets and had to borrow some CF-104s from other 1 CAG units for the Tiger Meet at Kleine Brogel in Belgium (*Andy Hodgson Collection*)

Royal Australian Navy

One of the lesser-known tiger squadrons, the sub-busters of the Royal
Australian Navy's VS-816 only ever attended one Tiger Meet: the 1977 event
at RAF Greenham Common in Berkshire. VS-816 operated Grumman Trackers
from NAS Nowra and were deployed on the aircraft carrier HMAS *Melbourne*.
The Trackers and the *Melbourne* are history now (*via Frank Visser*)